Knock-knock.
Who's there?
Aaron.
Aaron who?
Aaron my tires, gas in my tank...so let's go!

> Knock-knock.
> *Who's there?*
> Abbie.
> *Abbie who?*
> Abbie stung my big toe!

Knock-knock.
Who's there?
Ada.
Ada who?
Ada hamburger, yum-yum...want one?

Knock-knock.
Who's there?
Aisle.
Aisle who?
Aisle never tell your secret.

Knock-knock.
Who's there?
Alaska.
Alaska who?
Alaska, but I don't think Mom will let me bungee jump.

Knock-knock.
Who's there?
Aleta.
Aleta who?
Aleta whole pizza by myself.

Knock-knock.
Who's there?
Allison.
Allison who?
Allison Wonderland.

Knock-knock.
Who's there?
Althea.
Althea who?
Althea when I get out of
detention.

Knock-knock.
Who's there?
Ammonia.
Ammonia who?
Ammonia little kid, so I can't reach the doorbell.

Knock-knock.
Who's there?
Andrew.
Andrew who?
Andrew on the walls, and was her
mother mad!

Knock-knock.
Who's there?
Andy.
Andy who?
Andy huffed and he puffed and he blew my
house down!

Knock-knock.
Who's there?
Anita.
Anita who?
Anita shower, now!

Knock-knock.
Who's there?
Annapolis.
Annapolis who?
Annapolis is what you eat each day to keep the doctor away.

Knock-knock.
Who's there?
Anton.
Anton who?
Anton your potato salad. Don't worry, it won't eat much.

Knock-knock.
Who's there?
Appeal.
Appeal who?
Appeal is what covers a banana.

Knock-knock.
Who's there?
Archibald.
Archibald who?
Archibald, but he's buying a wig tomorrow.

Knock-knock.
Who's there?
Bacon.
Bacon who?
Bacon a chocolate cake for your birthday.

 Knock-knock.
 Who's there?
 Banana split.
 Banana split who?
 Banana split, so ice creamed!

Knock-knock.
Who's there?
Barry.
Barry who?
Barry rude of you not to answer the door.

Knock-knock.
Who's there?
Bearskin.
Bearskin who?
Bearskin hibernate in caves all winter.

8

Knock-knock.
  Who's there?
Bed.
  Bed who?
Bed you can't tell I've
got a code in my nose.

Knock-knock.
  Who's there?
Beehive.
  Beehive who?
Beehive yourself and
get buzzy!

Knock-knock.
  Who's there?
Ben Hur.
  Ben Hur who?
Ben Hur an hour. Let
me in!

Knock-knock.
  Who's there?
Ben and Anna.
  Ben and Anna who?
Ben and Anna split!

Knock-knock.
  Who's there?
Ben and Doris.
  Ben and Doris who?
Ben knocking all
morning—Doris stuck!

Knock-knock.
  Who's there?
Beth.
  Beth who?
Beth wishes on your
birthday, thweetheart.

Knock-knock.
    Who's there?
Bless.
    Bless who?
I don't know—I didn't sneeze.

Knock-knock.
    Who's there?
Boysenberry.
    Boysenberry who?
Boysenberry cute girls are all
invited to my party.

Knock-knock.
    Who's there?
Butternut.
    Butternut who?
Butternut try
to pick up a skunk.

Knock-knock.
Who's there?
Caesar.
Caesar who?
Caesar great homes for sharks and dolphins.

Knock-knock.
Who's there?
Cameron.
Cameron who?
Cameron film are all you need to take photos.

Knock-knock.
Who's there?
Candice.
Candice who?
Candice class get any more boring?

Knock-knock.
Who's there?
Cannelloni.
Cannelloni who?
Cannelloni some money until I get my allowance?

Knock-knock.
Who's there?
Candidate.
Candidate who?
Candidate be changed to Friday?

Knock-knock.
Who's there?
Canoe.
Canoe who?
Canoe please get off my foot?

Knock-knock.
Who's there?
Carmen.
Carmen who?
Carmen get it!
Dinner's ready!

Knock-knock.
Who's there?
Carrie.
Carrie who?
Carrie on with what
you're doing—I'm at
the wrong door.

Knock-knock.
Who's there?
Cash.
Cash who?
Cashew? That's my
favorite nut.

Knock-knock.
Who's there?
Catsup.
Catsup who?
Catsup on the roof.
Should I bring her
down?

Knock-knock.
Who's there?
Cattle.
Cattle who?
Cattle always purr
when you pet it.

Knock-knock.
Who's there?
Cecile.
Cecile who?
Cecile the d-door!
A m-monster's
outs-s-side!

Knock-knock.
Who's there?
Cher.
Cher who?
Cher your toys,
and you'll have lots of friends.

Knock-knock.
Who's there?
Chester.
Chester who?
Chester minute, pardner...
you new in this here town?

Knock-knock.
Who's there?
Cooper.
Cooper who?
Cooper chickens up before they run off!

Knock-knock.
Who's there?
Culver.
Culver who?
Culver up my feet—they're freezing!

Knock-knock.
Who's there?
Dandelion.
Dandelion who?
Dandelion always
growls at Tony the
tiger.

Knock-knock.
Who's there?
Danielle.
Danielle who?
Danielle so loud,
my ears hurt.

Knock-knock.
Who's there?
Daryl.
Daryl who?
Daryl never be anyone
as weird as you.

15

Knock-knock.
Who's there?
Debate.
Debate who?
Debate is what you use to catch de fish.

Knock-knock.
Who's there?
Deceit.
Deceit who?
Deceit of your jeans has a big hole.

Knock-knock.
Who's there?
Deduct.
Deduct who?
Deduct says, "Quack! Quack!"

Knock-knock.
Who's there?
Denise.
Denise who?
Denise are above de
ankles.

Knock-knock.
Who's there?
Dewey.
Dewey who?
Dewey really have to
go to school today?

Knock-knock.
Who's there?
Diana.
Diana who?
Diana thirst...got any
water?

Knock-knock.
Who's there?
Diego.
Diego who?
Diego before de B.

Knock-knock.
Who's there?
Diesel.
Diesel who?
Diesel teach you to fix
your doorbell.

Knock-knock.
    Who's there?
Dinah snores.
    Dinah snores who?
Dinah snores live in Jurassic Park.

Knock-knock.
    Who's there?
Dipsticks.
    Dipsticks who?
Dipsticks on my cracker when I dunk it in the bowl.

Knock-knock.
Who's there?
Disguise.
Disguise who?
Disguise killing me with all his corny jokes.

Knock-knock.
Who's there?
Dishes.
Dishes who?
Dishes the last time I eat anchovies for
breakfast.

Knock-knock.
Who's there?
Dish towel.
Dish towel who?
Dish towel is soaked. Would you get me a dry
one?

Knock-knock.
Who's there?
Dismay.
Dismay who?
Dismay not be a good time to knock.

Knock-knock.
Who's there?
Distress.
Distress who?
Distress makes me look like
an elephant in a tutu.

Knock-knock.
  Who's there?
Doctor Dolittle.
  Doctor Dolittle who?
Doctor Dolittle to cure my sore throat.

Knock-knock.
  Who's there?
Dogma.
  Dogma who?
Dogma best friend.

Knock-knock.
  Who's there?
Dumbbell.
  Dumbbell who?
Dumbbell doesn't work, so I had to knock.

Knock-knock.
  Who's there?
Eclipse.
  Eclipse who?
Eclipse his moustache when it curls over his mouth.

Knock-knock.
  Who's there?
Egg roll and sausage.
  Egg roll and sausage who?
Egg roll off the counter—I never sausage a mess!

Knock-knock.
  Who's there?
Eggshell.
  Eggshell who?
Eggshell be our breakfast tomorrow morning.

Knock-knock.
  Who's there?
Elaine.
  Elaine who?
Elaine down on the couch. Should I wake him up?

Knock-knock.
  Who's there?
Eliza.
  Eliza who?
Eliza lot, but sometimes he tells the truth.

Knock-knock.
Who's there?
Ellie Fence.
Ellie Fence who?
Ellie Fence never
forget.

Knock-knock.
Who's there?
Ellis.
Ellis who?
Ellis the letter that
comes before M.

Knock-knock.
Who's there?
Emerson.
Emerson who?
Emerson awesome
earrings you're
wearing.

Knock-knock.
Who's there?
Esau.
Esau who?
Esau a pitbull and
jumped back on his
bike.

Knock-knock.
Who's there?
Esme.
Esme who?
Esme shirt untucked?

Knock-knock.
Who's there?
Eyedrops.
Eyedrops who?
Eyedrops my keys, then I picks them up.

       Knock-knock.
          Who's there?
       Eyelashes.
          Eyelashes who?
       Eyelashes myself to the mast
       during a storm.

Knock-knock.
Who's there?
Ezra.
Ezra who?
Ezra a doctor in the house?

Knock-knock.
Who's there?
Farrah.
Farrah who?
Farrah way, I saw a
hot air balloon.

Knock-knock.
Who's there?
Fatima.
Fatima who?
Fatima stomach makes
my jeans tight.

Knock-knock.
Who's there?
Felice.
Felice who?
Felice is what sheep
grow on their skin.

Knock-knock.
  Who's there?
Felix.
  Felix who?
Felix my face, that dog is out of here!

Knock-knock.
  Who's there?
Fido.
  Fido who?
Fido known you were here, I would have phoned.

Knock-knock.
  Who's there?
Firewood.
  Firewood who?
Firewood sure make these marshmallows melt faster.

Knock-knock.
  Who's there?
Flora.
  Flora who?
Flora my room sure is a mess!

Knock-knock.
  Who's there?
Frieda.
  Frieda who?
Frieda cow! She's stuck in the fence!

Knock-knock.
  Who's there?
G. I.
  G. I. who?
G. I. wish I had a million bucks.

> Knock-knock.
>   *Who's there?*
> Galahad.
>   *Galahad who?*
> Galahad an ice cream cone, but she
> dropped it.

Knock-knock.
  Who's there?
Ghosts go.
  Ghosts go who?
No, silly. Ghosts go "Boo!"

Knock-knock.
  Who's there?
Gladys.
  Gladys who?
Gladys better than feeling sad.

Knock-knock.
  Who's there?
Goblin.
  Goblin who?
Goblin your dinner will give you a stomach ache.

Knock-knock.
   Who's there?
Goliath.
   Goliath who?
Goliath down, you
looketh sleepy.

Knock-knock.
   Who's there?
Gomez.
   Gomez who?
Gomez not allowed to
be chewed in class.

Knock-knock.
   Who's there?
Gopher.
   Gopher who?
Gopher pizza...I'll wait
here.

Knock-knock.
   Who's there?
Greta.
   Greta who?
Greta good grade on
that math test and
amaze your parents!

Knock-knock.
   Who's there?
Gruesome.
   Gruesome who?
Gruesome purple
petunias in my garden.

Knock-knock.
   Who's there?
Guest.
   Guest who?
Guest wrong, now I'll
have to take the math
test again.

Knock-knock.
   Who's there?
Gumby.
   Gumby who?
Gumby difficult to
scrape off the bottom
of your shoe.

Knock-knock.
Who's there?
Guru.
Guru who?
Guru two inches last year.

Knock-knock.
Who's there?
Gus.
Gus who?
Gus I'll have to come back later.

Knock-knock.
Who's there?
Gwen.
Gwen who?
Gwen fishing? Can I come?

Knock-knock.
Who's there?
Hairdo.
Hairdo who?
Hairdo a great job of keeping your head warm.

Knock-knock.
Who's there?
Hans.
Hans who?
Hans off my candy bar!

Knock-knock.
Who's there?
Harmony.
Harmony who?
Harmony times have I
asked you to open this
door!

Knock-knock.
Who's there?
Harris.
Harris who?
Harris in my eyes, so
I'd better use some gel.

Knock-knock.
Who's there?
Harry.
Harry who?
Harry up and answer
the door!

Knock-knock.
Who's there?
Harvey.
Harvey who?
Harvey having fun
yet?

Knock-knock.
Who's there?
Hatch-hatch-hatch.
*Hatch-hatch-hatch
who?*
Bless you! Need a
tissue?

Knock-knock.
Who's there?
Hayes.
Hayes who?
Hayes what horses eat.

Knock-knock.
  Who's there?
Henrietta.
  Henrietta who?
Henrietta healthy lunch.

Knock-knock.
  Who's there?
Hobbit.
  Hobbit who?
Hobbit your way, smarty-pants.

Knock-knock.
  Who's there?
Hogwash.
  Hogwash who?
Hogwash in our pool and muddied up the deck.

Knock-knock.
  Who's there?
Homer.
  Homer who?
Homer away, I always take a bath on
Saturday night.

Knock-knock.
  Who's there?
Honeycomb.
  Honeycomb who?
Honeycomb your hair before we go to the dance.

Knock-knock.
  Who's there?
Honeydew.
  Honeydew who?
Honeydew you like your pizza hot or
cold?

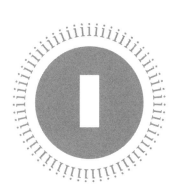

Knock-knock.
> *Who's there?*
Ice cream.
> *Ice cream who?*
Ice cream when I see vampires on TV.

Knock-knock.
> *Who's there?*
Icing.
> *Icing who?*
Icing a song for you on your birthday.

Knock-knock.
> *Who's there?*

Icon.
> *Icon who?*

Icon double-click my mouse faster than you can.

Knock-knock.
> *Who's there?*

Ida.
> *Ida who?*

Ida come earlier, but I crashed my skateboard.

Knock-knock.
> *Who's there?*

Imus.
> *Imus who?*

Imus get out of bed, or I'll be late for school.

Knock-knock.
> *Who's there?*

Income.
> *Income who?*

Income the cats if you leave the door open.

Knock-knock.
Who's there?
Intense.
Intense who?
Intense is where I like to sleep on camping trips.

Knock-knock.
Who's there?
Iona.
Iona who?
Iona new skateboard, nyah, nyah.

Knock-knock.
Who's there?
Iran.
Iran who?
Iran all the way to second base.

Knock-knock.
Who's there?
Iraq.
Iraq who?
Iraq my brain for math test answers.

Knock-knock.
Who's there?
Isabel.
Isabel who?
Isabel out of order? I had to knock.

Knock-knock.
Who's there?
Isadore.
Isadore who?
Isadore open? I'm freezing!

Knock-knock.
Who's there?
Isaiah.
Isaiah who?
Isaiah little prayer before I go to sleep.

Knock-knock.
Who's there?
Ivana.
Ivana who?
Ivana stick of gum.

Knock-knock.
Who's there?
Izzy.
Izzy who?
Izzy coming now, or isn't he?

Knock-knock.
> *Who's there?*
Jackal.
> *Jackal who?*
Jackal mow your lawn, if you pay him.

Knock-knock.
> *Who's there?*
Jean-Claude.
> *Jean-Claude who?*
Jean-Claude at the dirt as he slid into first base.

Knock-knock.
Who's there?
Jester.
Jester who?
Jester minute...I'm fixing your doorbell.

Knock-knock.
Who's there?
Jody.
Jody who?
Jody first guy to hit a homerun for de team.

Knock-knock.
Who's there?
Josie.
Josie who?
Josie his tent get trashed by a bear!

Knock-knock.
Who's there?
Juan.
Juan who?
Juan day soon I'll be able to drive.

Knock-knock.
Who's there?
Juanita.
Juanita who?
Juanita chocolate-covered ant?

Knock-knock.
Who's there?
Juicy.
Juicy who?
Juicy any ghosts
under my bed?

Knock-knock.
Who's there?
Juliet.
Juliet who?
Juliet birthday cake
at my party.

Knock-knock.
Who's there?
Junior.
Junior who?
Junior flowers come up; July they
bloom.

Knock-knock.
Who's there?
Juno.
Juno who?
Juno what time it is now?

Knock-knock.
Who's there?
Justice.
Justice who?
Justice I thought...your doorbell's broken.

Knock-knock.
Who's there?
Justin.
Justin who?
Justin the neighborhood and thought I'd say
hello.

Knock-knock.
Who's there?
Justina.
Justina who?
Justina nick of time, I caught my pet tarantula
before it escaped.

Knock-knock.
Who's there?
Kanga.
Kanga who?
Not kangawho, silly—kangaroo!

Knock-knock.
Who's there?
Katmandu.
Katmandu who?
Katmandu exactly what Catwoman do.

Knock-knock.
Who's there?
Keith.
Keith who?
Keith me, thweetheart.

Knock-knock.
Who's there?
Kent.
Kent who?
Kent go with you, I'm grounded.

Knock-knock.
Who's there?
Kenya.
Kenya who?
Kenya see my belly button in
these pants?

Knock-knock.
Who's there?
Kerry.
Kerry who?
Kerry me over the mud puddle,
will you?

Knock-knock.
Who's there?
Ketchup.
Ketchup who?
Ketchup to her before she dives
into that dumpster!

Knock-knock.
   Who's there?
Kiefer.
   Kiefer who?
Kiefer my door is lost.

Knock-knock.
   Who's there?
Kimmy.
   Kimmy who?
Kimmy a little kiss,
Sweetie.

Knock-knock.
   Who's there?
Kip.
   Kip who?
Kip your sneaky hands
out of my popcorn!

Knock-knock.
   Who's there?
Kitty litter.
   Kitty litter who?
Kitty litter mouse get
away!

Knock-knock.
  Who's there?
Kleenex.
  Kleenex who?
Kleenex look nicer than dirty necks.

Knock-knock.
  Who's there?
Knotty.
  Knotty who?
Knotty little kids get time out.

Knock-knock.
  Who's there?
Krakatoa.
  Krakatoa who?
Krakatoa on that darn cement step!

Knock-knock.
Who's there?
Lady.
Lady who?
Lady mat on the porch and I won't track mud in the house.

Knock-knock.
Who's there?
Landon.
Landon who?
Landon on your belly hurts!

Knock-knock.
Who's there?
Leda.
Leda who?
Leda horse to water but you can't make him drink.

Knock-knock.
Who's there?
Lena.
Lena who?
Lena little closer and I'll brush that man-eating spider off your shoulder.

Knock-knock.
Who's there?
Lettuce and beet.
Lettuce and beet who?
Lettuce stop this knocking...I'm beet.

Knock-knock.
Who's there?
Lettuce and turnips.
Lettuce and turnips who?
Lettuce see if any evidence turnips before we call the cops.

Knock-knock.
Who's there?
Lewis.
Lewis who?
Lewis too short to ride the roller coaster.

Knock-knock.
Who's there?
Linda.
Linda who?
Linda hand, please—I can't seem to open this door!

Knock-knock.
Who's there?
Lion.
Lion who?
Lion down for a nap.

Knock-knock.
Who's there?
Lionel.
Lionel who?
Lionel bite if you stick your hand in the cage.

Knock-knock.
　Who's there?
Lipstick.
　Lipstick who?
Lipstick together when
you blow bubblegum.

Knock-knock.
　Who's there?
Lucy.
　Lucy who?
Lucy trousers fally
down.

Knock-knock.
　Who's there?
Luke.
　Luke who?
Luke through the
keyhole and you
might find out.

Knock-knock.
　Who's there?
Luther.
　Luther who?
Luther jeans would fit
me much better.

Knock-knock.
　Who's there?
Lydia.
　Lydia who?
Lydia teapot is
cracked.

Knock-knock.
Who's there?
Macaw.
Macaw who?
Macaw won't start. Can you give me a lift?

Knock-knock.
Who's there?
Mackie.
Mackie who?
Mackie roni and cheese.

Knock-knock.
Who's there?
Major.
Major who?
Major answer the door, didn't I?

Knock-knock.
Who's there?
Mandissa.
Mandissa who?
Mandissa great place for a picnic.

Knock-knock.
Who's there?
Mandy.
Mandy who?
Mandy lifeboats—we've hit an iceberg!

Knock-knock.
Who's there?
Marcus.
Marcus who?
Marcus down for two
tickets, please.

Knock-knock.
Who's there?
Marmalade.
Marmalade who?
Marmalade an egg.

Knock-knock.
Who's there?
Maura.
Maura who?
Maura those French fries
and another burger, please.

Knock-knock.
Who's there?
Maya.
Maya who?
Maya good joke teller?

Knock-knock.
Who's there?
Meat patty.
Meat patty who?
Meat Patty, then meet
her brother Frank Furter.

Knock-knock.
Who's there?
Mia.
Mia who?
Mia genius; you a
dummy.

Knock-knock.
Who's there?
Moira.
Moira who?
Moira that birthday
cake, please.

Knock-knock.
Who's there?
Momma.
Momma who?
Momma good cook.

Knock-knock.
Who's there?
Musket.
Musket who?
Musket a job—I'm
broke.

Knock-knock.
Who's there?
Myth.
Myth who?
Myth my two fwont
teefth in my mowfth.

Knock-knock.
Who's there?
Nadia.
Nadia who?
Nadia head if you understand the question.

Knock-knock.
Who's there?
Nanny.
Nanny who?
Nanny one going to answer this door?

Knock-knock.
Who's there?
Nantucket.
Nantucket who?
Nantucket, but she'll give it right back.

Knock-knock.
Who's there?
Napkin.
Napkin who?
Napkin pep you up if you don't snooze too long.

Knock-knock.
Who's there?
Needle.
Needle who?
Needle little sympathy.

Knock-knock.
Who's there?
Nickel.
Nickel who?
Nickel dance the hula if we buy him a grass skirt.

Knock-knock.
Who's there?
Noah.
Noah who?
Noah good place to find more jokes?

Knock-knock.
Who's there?
Noggin.
Noggin who?
Noggin on your door for about an hour now.

Knock-knock.
Who's there?
Nonna.
Nonna who?
Nonna your business who I am.

Knock-knock.
Who's there?
Norma Lee.
Norma Lee who?
Norma Lee I rinse my mouth
after the dog kisses me.

Knock-knock.
Who's there?
Norway.
Norway who?
Norway am I going to
open this door.

Knock-knock.
Who's there?
Nosey.
Nosey who?
Nosey can't get in,
so he's going to get a key.

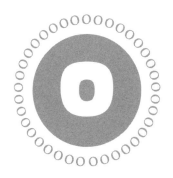

Knock-knock.
  Who's there?
Oil.
  Oil who?
Oil see you later, alligator.

Knock-knock.
  Who's there?
Oink-oink.
  Oink-oink who?
Make up your mind...are you a pig or an owl?

Knock-knock.
Who's there?
Olaf.
Olaf who?
Olaf if you tickle my feet.

Knock-knock.
Who's there?
Olive.
Olive who?
Olive on Maple Street. Where do you live?

Knock-knock.
Who's there?
Oliver.
Oliver who?
Oliver clothes got wet when she
fell into the pool.

Knock-knock.
Who's there?
Ollie.
Ollie who?
Ollie your teeth are green!
Don't you brush?

Knock-knock.
Who's there?
Oman.
Oman who?
Oman, are you cute!

Knock-knock.
Who's there?
Omelet and butter.
Omelet and butter who?
Omelet stronger than I look, so
you butter watch out.

Knock-knock.
Who's there?
Osborn.
Osborn who?
Osborn in a hospital.
Where's you born?

Knock-knock.
Who's there?
Oslo.
Oslo who?
Oslo down for squirrels.

Knock-knock.
   Who's there?
Oswald.
   Oswald who?
Oswald my bubblegum!

       Knock-knock.
          Who's there?
       Owl.
          Owl who?
       Owl tell you a secret if you don't
       blab it around.

Knock-knock.
   Who's there?
Oz.
   Oz who?
Oz got to sneeze! Stand back!

       Knock-knock.
          Who's there?
       Ozzie.
          Ozzie who?
       Ozzie you when you get back.

Knock-knock.
Who's there?
Panther.
Panther who?
Panther no panth, I'm going thwimming.

Knock-knock.
Who's there?
Paradise.
Paradise who?
Paradise are all you need to play board games.

Knock-knock.
  Who's there?
Pecan.
  Pecan who?
Pecan somebody your own size!

Knock-knock.
  Who's there?
Peeka.
  Peeka who?
Not peeka who, silly...peekaboo.

Knock-knock.
  Who's there?
Phyllis.
  Phyllis who?
Phyllis in on the latest gossip.

Knock-knock.
  Who's there?
Pickle.
  Pickle who?
Pickle work better than a shovel
in your garden.

Knock-knock.
  Who's there?
Piggyback.
  Piggyback who?
Piggyback home before
the Big Bad Wolf
could catch it.

Knock-knock.
Who's there?
Pink panther.
Pink panther who?
Pink panther more girlish than blue panth.

Knock-knock.
Who's there?
Pizza.
Pizza who?
Pizza nice guy when you get to know him.

Knock-knock.
Who's there?
Plato.
Plato who?
Plato nachos, please.

Knock-knock.
Who's there?
Police.
Police who?
Police let me in! There's a hurricane out here!

Knock-knock.
Who's there?
Poodle.
Poodle who?
Poodle little chow in Fido's dish, will you?

Knock-knock.
Who's there?
Popcan.
Popcan who?
Popcan make you burp if you drink it too fast.

Knock-knock.
Who's there?
Pudding.
Pudding who?
Pudding your hand in a crocodile's mouth is really dumb.

Knock-knock.
Who's there?
Punch.
Punch who?
Not me!

Knock-knock.
Who's there?
Q-T.
Q-T who?
Q-T pie, you're
adorable.

Knock-knock.
Who's there?
Q-tip.
Q-tip who?
Q-tip over when you
do a handstand?

Knock-knock.
Who's there?
Quacker.
Quacker who?
Quacker cwumbs are in my bed.

Knock-knock.
Who's there?
Quacks.
Quacks who?
Quacks in the ground come
from earthquacks.

Knock-knock.
Who's there?
Queen.
Queen who?
Queen up your room, please.

Knock-knock.
Who's there?
Queue.
Queue who?
Queue better floss that spinach
out of your teeth.

Knock-knock.
Who's there?
Raisin.
Raisin who?
Raisin chickens is a cheep-cheep job.

Knock-knock.
Who's there?
Razor.
Razor who?
Razor hand if you have the correct answer.

Knock-knock.
Who's there?
Ringo.
Ringo who?
Ringo on the bride's finger.

Knock-knock.
Who's there?
Robin.
Robin who?
Robin the cookie jar again?

Knock-knock.
Who's there?
Rocco.
Rocco who?
Rocco-bye baby, on the treetop....

Knock-knock.
Who's there?
Ron.
Ron who?
Ron faster! There's a tyrannosaurus after us!

Knock-knock.
  Who's there?
Sadie.
  Sadie who?
Sadie magic word, and I'll pass the nuts.

  Knock-knock.
    Who's there?
  Salmon and porpoise.
    Salmon and porpoise who?
  Salmon Alex swam with a dolphin,
  but they didn't do it on porpoise.

Knock-knock.
Who's there?
Samoa.
Samoa who?
Samoa that super-sized soda will give me the hiccups.

Knock-knock.
Who's there?
Sasha.
Sasha who?
Sasha lot of silly questions!

Knock-knock.
Who's there?
Santa.
Santa who?
Santa e-mail to you but you never replied.

Knock-knock.
Who's there?
Selma.
Selma who?
Selma bike, then I'll buy a scooter.

Knock-knock.
  Who's there?
Senior.
  Senior who?
Senior boa constrictor around here lately?

Knock-knock.
  Who's there?
Sharon.
  Sharon who?
Sharon my pizza is not what I had in mind.

Knock-knock.
  Who's there?
Sherwood.
  Sherwood who?
Sherwood be more fun if my skateboard had wheels.

Knock-knock.
  Who's there?
Shirley.
  Shirley who?
Shirley you must know where I left my homework.

Knock-knock.
   Who's there?
Sid.
   Sid who?
Sid down and speak up.

Knock-knock.
   Who's there?
Ski tow.
   Ski tow who?
Ski tow bites itch like crazy.

Knock-knock.
   Who's there?
Snow.
   Snow who?
Snow body but me knows who Santa really is.

Knock-knock.
   Who's there?
Sonia.
   Sonia who?
Sonia matter of time before I turn into a werewolf.

Knock-knock.
   Who's there?
Spell.
   Spell who?
W-H-O.

Knock-knock.
   Who's there?
Statue.
   Statue who?
Statue who burped just now?

Knock-knock.
Who's there?
Talia.
Talia who?
Talia a bedtime story if you put your jammies on.

Knock-knock.
Who's there?
Tamara.
Tamara who?
Tamara is Saturday; today is Friday.

Knock-knock.
Who's there?
Tara.
Tara who?
Tara hole in your T-shirt?

Knock-knock.
Who's there?
Tarzan.
Tarzan who?
Tarzan stripes decorate flags of many nations.

Knock-knock.
Who's there?
Teddy bear.
Teddy bear who?
Teddy bear because he's taking a bath.

Knock-knock.
Who's there?
Knock-knock.
Who's there?
Thesis.
Thesis who?
Thesis the last time
I'm knocking!

Knock-knock.
Who's there?
Thumb.
Thumb who?
Thumb like it hot,
thumb like it cold.

Knock-knock.
Who's there?
Thistle.
Thistle who?
Thistle be me—
who are you?

Knock-knock.
Who's there?
Thumping.
Thumping who?
Thumping gooey is
dripping down your
chin.

Knock-knock.
Who's there?
Throat.
Throat who?
Throat to me, and I'll
score a touchdown.

Knock-knock.
Who's there?
Tilda.
Tilda who?
Tilda sun rises, I'll be
doing my homework.

Knock-knock.
Who's there?
Tom Sawyer.
Tom Sawyer who?
Tom Sawyer underwear in gym class.

Knock-knock.
Who's there?
Tooth.
Tooth who?
Tooth company, threeth a crowd.

Knock-knock.
Who's there?
Tuba.
Tuba who?
Tuba toothpaste makes my teeth sparkle.

Knock-knock.
Who's there?
Tulips.
Tulips who?
Tulips kiss better than one lip.

Knock-knock.
Who's there?
U-2.
U-2 who?
U-2 can be a rock star in ten easy lessons!

Knock-knock.
Who's there?
U-4.
U-4 who?
U-4 me, and me for you.

Knock-knock.
Who's there?
Ubangi.
Ubangi who?
Ubangi on my door
one more time and
you're history!

Knock-knock.
Who's there?
UCI.
UCI who?
UCI had to knock
because your doorbell
doesn't work.

Knock-knock.
Who's there?
Udder.
Udder who?
Udder joke's better
than this one.

Knock-knock.
Who's there?
Uganda.
Uganda who?
Uganda lot of weight
over vacation.

Knock-knock.
Who's there?
Uma.
Uma who?
Uma good buddy.

Knock-knock.
Who's there?
Unaware.
Unaware who?
Unaware sticking
out of your jeans!

Knock-knock.
Who's there?
Unit.
Unit who?
Unit me a sweater,
and I'll knit you
some mittens.

Knock-knock.
Who's there?
Urchin.
Urchin who?
Urchin sticks out
below her teeth.

Knock-knock.
   Who's there?
Uriah.
   Uriah who?
Uriah looks bloodshot.

Knock-knock.
   Who's there?
Uruguay.
   Uruguay who?
Uruguay who knows how to treat a gwirl.

Knock-knock.
   Who's there?
Usher.
   Usher who?
Usher up...she's singing too loud.

Knock-knock.
Who's there?
Vanessa.
Vanessa who?
Vanessa bus coming?

Knock-knock.
Who's there?
Venice.
Venice who?
Venice your next birthday?

Knock-knock.
Who's there?
Vera.
Vera who?
Vera interesting...can you repeat that?

Knock-knock.
Who's there?
Viper.
Viper who?
Viper nose before it drips on her T-shirt.

Knock-knock.
Who's there?
Vlad.
Vlad who?
Vlad to meet you, Count Dracula.

Knock-knock.
Who's there?
Voodoo.
Voodoo who?
Voodoo you think you're kidding?

Knock-knock.
Who's there?
W.
W who?
W, and your clone can answer the door!

Knock-knock.
Who's there?
Waddle.
Waddle who?
Waddle you do if I knock again?

Knock-knock.
Who's there?
Wayne.
Wayne who?
Wayne is falling on
my pawade.

Knock-knock.
Who's there?
Wes.
Wes who?
Wes the exit? I'm lost!

Knock-knock.
Who's there?
Weasel.
Weasel who?
Weasel for your dog,
and maybe she'll come
home.

Knock-knock.
Who's there?
Whale.
Whale who?
Whale I'll be a
monkey's uncle!

Knock-knock.
Who's there?
Wendy.
Wendy who?
Wendy moon comes
up, de sun goes down.

Knock-knock.
Who's there?
Who.
Who who?
Do you hear an owl
around here?

Knock-knock.
Who's there?
Why do owls go.
Why do owls go who?
Because that's how they talk, silly!

Knock-knock.
Who's there?
Wiggle.
Wiggle who?
Wiggle fall off your head if the wind blows hard.

Knock-knock.
Who's there?
Wire.
Wire who?
Wire you asking? It's me, knucklehead.

Knock-knock.
Who's there?
Witches.
Witches who?
Witches the one you want? This one or that?

Knock-knock.
Who's there?
Wooden shoe.
Wooden shoe who?
Wooden shoe like to sleep over?

Knock-knock.
Who's there?
Wonton.
Wonton who?
Wonton more pizza than you can eat is a waste of food.

Knock-knock.
Who's there?
Woodchuck.
Woodchuck who?
Woodchuck mow the lawn if we paid him?

Knock-knock.
   Who's there?
X.
   X who?
X and bacon are my favorite breakfast foods.

Knock-knock.
   Who's there?
XL.
   XL who?
XL at sports and you'll be famous.

Knock-knock.
Who's there?
Xavier.
Xavier who?
Xavier ticket stubs and win a prize!

Knock-knock.
Who's there?
Xenia.
Xenia who?
Xenia at the mall, but you didn't see me.

Knock-knock.
Who's there?
Xerox.
Xerox who?
Xerox fell on my head when I went mountain climbing.

Knock-knock.
Who's there?
Xs.
Xs who?
Xs are used by lumberjacks to cut down trees.

Knock-knock.
Who's there?
Yaw.
Yaw who?
Giddyap! Ride 'em, cowboy!

Knock-knock.
Who's there?
Yoda.
Yoda who?
Yoda man.

Knock-knock.
Who's there?
Yolanda.
Yolanda who?
Yolanda plane on the runway.

Knock-knock.
Who's there?
Yoo.
Yoo who?
Yoo-hoo, yourself.

Knock-knock.
Who's there?
Yukon.
Yukon who?
Yukon come with us if you pay your share.

Knock-knock.
Who's there?
Yule.
Yule who?
Yule be sorry if you miss Santa.

Knock-knock.
Who's there?
Yuma.
Yuma who?
Yuma very best friend.

Knock-knock.
Who's there?
Yvonne.
Yvonne who?
Yvonne my own mother doesn't recognize me with this wig on.

Knock-knock.
  Who's there?
Zany.
  Zany who?
Zany body home?

Knock-knock.
  Who's there?
Zelda.
  Zelda who?
Zelda bike to my neighbor.

Knock-knock.
Who's there?
Zenia.
Zenia who?
Zenia citizens get in
for half price.

Knock-knock.
Who's there?
Zeno.
Zeno who?
Zeno evil, hear no evil,
speak no evil.

Knock-knock.
Who's there?
Zeus.
Zeus who?
Zeus are where wild
animals are caged.

Knock-knock.
Who's there?
Zing.
Zing who?
Zing zome zongs with
me, okay?

Knock-knock.
Who's there?
Zoom.
Zoom who?
Zoom did you expect?

Knock-knock.
Who's there?
Zounds.
Zounds who?
Zounds! Zounds like this
might be the last joke.
It is!